OVERCOME PROCRASTINATION

How to be More Productive and Improve Time
Management - Your Tiny Productivity and Procrastination
Workbook

DANE A. GOLD

Cover Design by Teofan Gavriliu

The Icons used in this work were designed by:

- Flaticon, Freepik, classicvector, pikisuperstar, vectorjuice, ayunannas, pch.vector, and stories.

Published by Admore Publishing: Berlin, Germany

Printed in the United States of America

www.admorepublishing.com

Contents

An Introduction to Procrastination

"I stared in front of me at the blank document on my laptop screen. As I saw my reflection gazing back at me, I gave myself a motivational nod and thought, *okay, just let the words stream out of you.*"

This is how a good friend of mine, Brittney, described her first foray into writing a book. She is an incredibly talented personal trainer and health coach that encompasses everything in regards to healthy living. Brittney is so passionate about sharing good and helpful information in a space that is ravaged by misinformation and marketing techniques. Yet, she was having a tough time staying focused and starting on this new journey. She went on to explain a common scenario...

"As I was sitting there, excited about making a plan and an outline, a small Instagram icon popped up on my phone as it buzzed. I thought, okay, before I really get started, let me have a quick look."

I think we all know where this is headed and have been in the exact same situation as Brittney.

"Before I knew it, I looked up at the time, and I was an hour and a half into an endless Instagram wormhole of scrolling, double-tapping, and giggling at funny cat videos..."

What Brittney described to me was one of the many ways we all often procrastinate. Although it's clear that we do this to ourselves, it's still something we can't seem to stop doing. Procrastinating can feel harmless, and usually, everything works out alright.

Brittney has gone on to successfully write and publish 3 books, with more to come.

Still, it can be incredibly frustrating that we put ourselves through this. Procrastinating can also, however, have more severe consequences.

We often hear and tell ourselves, *there is always tomorrow*. It's a comforting thought, isn't it?

But the truth is, there isn't. Or at least, one day, there won't be.

We have no idea how long we will be on the planet or when our last today will be. We all hope it will be a long time in the future, but the truth is, no one knows for certain.

But it's not just life and death that is finite (and apologies for the heavy dose of existential angst!)

Even though we don't have hard deadlines or confirmed end dates for many things, nearly everything in your life will have a last day. There will be a last day of many relationships. You may or may not know when it will happen, but most will end at some point.

There will be a last day of most jobs you have. Again, you may or may not control when that happens, but most of them will end at some point.

If you have big dreams, whether it's to complete a specific degree, learn to play a particular sport, write a book, or backpack through Europe, there is an optimal window during which you can get them done. Putting these big dreams and goals off can mean you never achieve them at all.

If you are a parent, you have probably realized that there are plenty of lasts in your children's lives. The last time they say a particular word in a certain way. The last time they want to snuggle while you read them a story. The last time you have to wash their hair for them.

Change happens slowly, and we convince ourselves that there's always more time left to do the important stuff. But the truth is, telling ourselves that is more about allowing ourselves not to seize those opportunities. In the case of your children, though, how would you feel if you missed one of those 'lasts?'"

That's why, while it may be comfortable to put things off and promise ourselves that we'll do it soon, or tomorrow, or next week, often, the best time to tackle anything is today. Even when the stakes aren't as high as missing a big moment with a child or failing to take advantage of opportunities, procrastination can seriously and negatively impact our lives.

We tell ourselves that we'll start eating healthier next week. But before we know it, this turns into next month. Suddenly, it takes a severe wake-up call, like developing a condition such as diabetes or something even worse, before we take action.

We avoid tough conversations about our romantic relationships, so we have to put up with bad behavior or situations that either don't make us happy or actively make us miserable.

Work. Financial planning. Health. Love. Family. Everything vital, when we put it off, we risk losing the window of opportunity.

The fascinating thing is, putting things off until "tomorrow" or some other time in the future isn't exactly like saying we won't do it. *So, we can forgive ourselves and be flexible with a clear conscience.* Unfortunately, this magical tomorrow doesn't come until the stakes are much higher in many cases, and the consequences are much more severe. If at all.

Anyone who has ever burned the midnight oil cramming for an exam or panicked about getting a work project done in a quarter of the time required to do it well will know. But somehow, even though we know that putting things off will only make them worse, we still do it.

Procrastination is an easy and convenient way to lie to ourselves. Instead of being honest about not wanting to do something for whatever reason, we allow ourselves to believe that we'll just get it done tomorrow. Then tomorrow becomes the day after, and then next week, and before we know it, we're out of time, stressed out, and worried that the hammer is about to fall!

We procrastinate because we don't want to do something. Sometimes it's because it's too difficult. Sometimes we don't enjoy it. Often, we didn't want to do it in the first place and only said yes because we were too scared to say no. Whatever the reason, procrastination only leads to more stress, adverse outcomes, and potentially severe consequences.

No problem has ever been solved by putting it off.

The clock is always ticking, and as they say, "he who hesitates is lost."

The Story of the Procrastinator

If you're reading this, either you are a procrastinator yourself, or someone you know is. Either way, you're looking for a way to "cure" the problem of putting things off. You're in the right place.

Procrastination seems harmless enough. Putting something aside for a day or two while you take care of more pressing (or enjoyable) tasks doesn't seem like the worst thing you could ever do. But the trouble is, a day or two never really does it, and most people who procrastinate will put things off until the very last possible second. If they ever get done at all.

Have you ever known someone who is always planning to start a new diet, next week? Or the smoker who assures you that they'll have their last cigarette ever... after they finish the next pack. Maybe someone you know has a big dream to write a book or take a course, but while they talk about it all the time, they never actually take the first, crucial step?

Maybe you're that person.

We procrastinators usually aren't lazy or bad people. We just lack assertiveness and motivation. Procrastinators will often surround themselves with people who will enable and excuse their procrastination (or at least forgive them every time they do!) Even when you know, deep down, that putting things off was entirely within your control and the root cause of your problem, they'll stand by you and tell you everything is fine.

They also aren't necessary not successful. Many successful people still struggle with procrastination. They're just exceptional enough to be able to get things done despite themselves.

Procrastination often starts early in childhood or the teens and can be a lifelong problem. But it doesn't have to be, and there are steps everyone can take to break this cycle.

Making the Change

Like everything worth doing in life, ending your tendency to procrastinate takes a lot of will power. You have to recognize that it's a problem, commit to making a change, and find ways to force yourself to change the habit.

But, like any habit, being a procrastinator is one that can be broken. You can take steps to figure out why you procrastinate and create successful strategies to break the cycle.

In this book, we will look at why you might be procrastinating and look at the benefits and pitfalls you may be facing. We'll look at the cost of procrastination in various areas of your life and why it's crucial to take timely action.

Like everything in life, breaking a lifelong procrastination habit is not an overnight thing, so we'll also show you how to speak to the people in your life, get them on board, and help them to help you become accountable.

The good news is that you CAN stop procrastinating. Even if you put things off because you just have too much to cope with, there are strategies you can use to stop taking on so much and make it easier to get everything done before it becomes a crisis. It takes work, but there's no time like the present!

Reading this book is a great start, though! It means you've recognized that you might have a problem and that you need to work on it. As with anything, knowing why you do this is the first step. Then you need to learn small, easy-to-manage steps you can take to make the change, so keep reading, and let's get started!

Why Me?

In my case, when it comes to procrastinating, I know from personal experience. Like everyone, I've had moments where I have procrastinated before and where I suffered negative consequences. Everyone does it sometimes, and if they say they don't, they haven't done enough in their life!

But unlike most people who struggle with procrastination, I wanted to know why I do this and how I can avoid it, so I've put in the work. I started by examining my own motivation, so I knew why I was putting things off. Then I consulted many books, studies, websites, and documentaries to find out more about how ordinary people can take manageable steps to curb their desire to stall things.

I've created successful strategies that help me stay on task, minimize other reasons I used to procrastinate, and recognize when I am doing precisely that.

Of course, like everyone, I still slip up sometimes, and you will too. That's perfectly okay. It took you a lifetime to learn this habit, so you won't break it overnight. The important thing is never to stop trying. Even if you "fall off the wagon," you can keep working towards your goal.

You could read all the books, take all the courses, and join all the support groups too, but this book hopes to distill it all into one easy-to-use reference. Which is great, because if you're procrastinating, you might already have too much on your plate!

What This Book Is, and Is Not

This book is a guide designed to help you recognize why you might be procrastinating and develop strategies that help you break the pattern.

It's not a one size fits all solution. There are almost undoubtedly personal reasons that you procrastinate that will not be covered here. This is not supposed to be a rigid recipe for changing one way of thinking, but a road map to figure out what your thinking is and learn to take new roads.

Everyone has slightly different reasons for doing everything we do, and that's what makes us all unique and interesting. But it also means that you might need to adapt strategies to suit your specific needs and reasoning, and that's perfectly okay.

Not to mention that very often, it's rigid rules and strict requirements that make people who procrastinate rebel. I don't want to tell you what you must do. I just want to show you how you might do things a little better, to reduce your stress and improve your outcomes.

Also, this book is split up into 3 main parts, "What is Procrastination?", "Strategies to Deal with Procrastination", and lastly, "Maintenance". It was designed to be read from start to finish; however, if you are looking directly for solutions, you can jump straight to part II, "Strategies to Deal with Procrastination". There is nothing wrong with skimming through sections and picking up exactly what you need.

And so, without further delay, let's get to the meat and potatoes of it.

PROCRASTINATION
IS, HANDS DOWN,
OUR FAVORITE
FORM OF
SELF-SABOTAGE.

- Alyce P. Cornyn-Selby

What is Procrastination?

PART 1

"If you know the enemy and know yourself, you need not fear the result of a hundred battles. If you know yourself but not the enemy, for every victory gained you will also suffer a defeat. If you know neither the enemy nor yourself, you will succumb in every battle." Sun Tzu, The Art of War.

Yes, it may be a little dramatic to quote an ancient Chinese general in a book about procrastination, but that doesn't make it any less true.

In order to conquer anything, including procrastination, you first need to know both your enemy (or the problem you want to solve) and yourself (which we will get to in the next chapter.)

For now, let's take a closer look at what procrastination is and how it may be affecting your life.

ONE

What is This Procrastination Thing?

Let's be clear: everyone gets busy. Everyone has to prioritize things to give themselves a chance to get everything done. Many people have to delegate because they just have so much on the go.

But if you are consistently putting things aside and inventing reasons not to get to it, you are procrastinating.

Procrastination is not about being genuinely too busy to get to something, it's about consistently bumping it down the to-do list in favor of other things. It's about knowing that it's important and that there's a deadline looming and still convincing yourself to do something else.

What Is Procrastination?

procrastinate

<u>verb</u>

pro · cras · ti · nate | \ prə-ˈkra-stə-ˌnāt

*, prō- *

procrastinated, procrastinating

Definition of procrastinate

<u>transitive verb</u>

: to put off intentionally and habitually

<u>intransitive verb</u>

: to put off intentionally the doing of something that should be done

Most people procrastinate from time to time. It's human nature, and if it's occasional, it's not going to have a significant impact on your life.

The key words in the definition of procrastination are, *intentionally* and *habitually*.

If you're occasionally missing deadlines or not completing tasks because you're just too busy, you're not really procrastinating. You just need to reexamine your capabilities and scale back on responsibilities.

But if you find that you frequently don't deliver on particular kinds of tasks or responsibilities, or you find yourself rationalizing why you should do other things first, that's procrastination.

Doing this occasionally, with things that won't have a big impact on your life isn't the end of the world. But if you are frequently damaging your reputation at work, your chances at college, or the happiness and stability of your home life and relationships, you have a procrastination problem, and you need to take action.

My Story

I didn't spend a lot of time reading about and researching procrastination because I felt like it. I discovered that I genuinely had a problem with procrastination in my life.

It wasn't until I took a long, honest look at the patterns in my life that I realized that I was sacrificing my success and happiness by delaying things. I spent a lot of time looking for answers about why I (and others) do this and what the most common types of procrastination are.

Like many negative personality traits and behaviors, I will never 100% not be a procrastinator. But now that I know how to recognize the signs and take appropriate steps, I can better manage it. That's what I want to offer you too.

Even though I have learned to push myself to get things done and duck situations where I might want to avoid a project or task, I still have to be very careful.

The truth is, most people procrastinate about some things, sometimes. It's human nature to try to avoid things that make us uncomfortable, that we think might be difficult, or that we don't think we can do properly. It's normal to feel that way, but as they say, growth happens outside your comfort zone.

In the Beginning

If you are a procrastinator, there's a very good chance it's not something that happened overnight.

Most of us developed this behavior early in our lives. Probably even when we were in school and college.

Think back to your early years. Try to remember specific cases where you put things off that could and should have been done earlier. Maybe you waited until the last possible minute to work on school projects and assignments.

Perhaps you were the kid who crammed for exams the day before you had to write them.

The thing is, many people who are lifelong procrastinators did do that, and because they are often quite intelligent and capable people, for a long time, it probably worked just fine.

While other people were steadfastly doing their coursework and getting things done, you discovered that you could leave things to the last minute and get by. So, you spent time hanging out with friends, playing games, or spending hours on social media, knowing that you could still "phone it in" at the last minute and get by.

Unfortunately, the older you get, and the more critical the tasks are, the harder it gets to cram everything you should have been doing for weeks or months into a few days. At this point, you may not always get the results you need.

The problem is, by the time you realize this, procrastination may already have become a habit. You might be used to having everything your way – with all the free time you get from putting things off and still getting things done satisfactorily.

Whether this is comparable to your story, or you first started procrastinating later, the payoff is the same. You can do more of the things you like for longer and only worry about responsibilities and deadlines when they're hanging over your head.

You start to think of this as a "win-win" situation, and it becomes your subconscious strategy for everything.

The Cost of Procrastination

Payoffs are great. It's why we do pretty much everything.

We're like mice in a lab maze, running around, doing the scientists bidding, with the promise of cheese at the end of it all. Except as humans, we do things for money, power, prestige, admiration, love, and similar payoffs.

Everyone has different motivations, but they're all things that make us feel good, directly or indirectly.

When it comes to procrastinating, the payoff is having more time to do the things we want to do while still managing to deliver the things we must do. Sounds great, right?

But eventually, when you procrastinate, you start pushing your own limits, piling up too many things. You miss the deadlines. You don't deliver the results. You don't resolve the problem. And when that happens, you start having to deal with the costs of procrastinating.

If you're still studying, and procrastination is a problem, you may experience several negative consequences when things start catching up with you:

- You may take longer to complete courses.
- Your results may not be as good as they could have been.
- If you have to repeat courses or get more credits, it can cost you more money.
- If you struggle to complete your course, it may reflect poorly on you and limit future opportunities.

We don't only procrastinate when we're studying, though. Most people who start procrastinating in school and college continue the pattern. In an employment setting, this might mean:

- Less successful projects.
- Missed deadlines.
- Poor performance reviews.
- Fewer promotion opportunities.

In fact, if you procrastinate too much at work, it can lead to losing your job in extreme cases. It's important to note, though, that if you are procrastinating because you're just too swamped at work, you need to be proactive and seek help from your employer before any of these things happen. There are only so many hours in the day, and if you're having to triage work, you probably have too much to do.

It's not only our education and professional lives that can be damaged by procrastination, though. If you have a habit of putting things off rather than tackling them in a timely manner, then you may find it spills into your personal life. This may mean things like:

- Not seeking medical attention for health worries when they are mild, and then having to deal with more severe consequences.
- Failing to address relationship issues with your partner, spouse, or family, which can result in resentment and relationship breakdown.
- Not prioritizing your health, putting off diet and exercise, and then suffering health consequences.
- Putting off personal dreams and passions, believing there will always be time to tackle them in the future.

The truth is, as I mentioned when we started working on this, the only day that is absolutely guaranteed is today, and it's our job to "seize the day." So *carpe diem*, and let's discover how we talk ourselves into procrastinating.

The Internal Lie

As much as we like to think of ourselves as honest, the truth is, most people lie all the time.

We lie to spare people's feelings. For instance, telling our coworker we love their new shoes when we categorically don't.

We lie to make life easier for ourselves. By telling our friends we're busy, for example, when they're moving to a new house, so we can stay home and watch Netflix.

We even lie to our children by telling them that Santa is real. We don't mean to hurt them, but we do it anyway, to protect them and give them a hint of magic in their lives.

Procrastination is very much an internal lie that we tell ourselves.

When we put something aside to do it "tomorrow," we probably fully intend to do it then. But we also know that if something else were to come up in the meantime, tomorrow might very well become next week, or next month, or never.

We tell ourselves this lie for the same reasons we tell all the other lies we do: to take away anxiety and make ourselves feel good. We're not lazy or incapable. We're just putting this off for a little while, and then we'll get right on it.

The lie makes us feel better right now, which plays right into our love of instant gratification. Still, it doesn't solve the problem, and we're only postponing the negative consequences.

Procrastination makes us feel better in the moment, but it's like buying contentment on credit. Sometime soon, the bill will be due, and you're going to have to pay it with interest.

The good news is that you can start to change the pattern when you know why you are setting yourself up like this. Which is the very next thing we will be covering.

Self-Reflection

What does procrastination mean to me?

How do I typically procrastinate?

TOMORROW IS
OFTEN THE
BUSIEST DAY OF
THE WEEK.

- Spanish Proverb

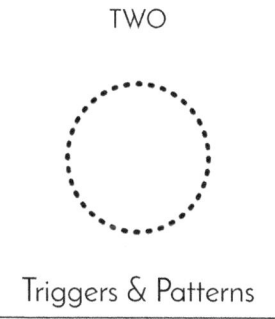

TWO

Triggers & Patterns

Most people never stop to think about why they do the things they do. But it's rarely up to chance.

Even if you think you are unpredictable, you aren't.

Everything in our lives combines to create our personality, and our personality is a blueprint for how we approach the world and our lives. Your choices, actions, and inactions are all a reflection of things that have happened to you and how you processed them.

The problem is very few of us ever really consider why we do the things we do, and without knowing the cause, it's tough to get to a solution.

You might think that procrastination is a simple problem, and to a degree, it is. But without knowing what is causing you to behave this way, it's almost impossible to change the way you act. So, this chapter is all about some of the reasons why people procrastinate. You may recognize your-self in more than one of these, and that's normal too. But finding the reasons why YOU procrastinate is the first step in finding effective strategies to break the habit.

The Pattern of Procrastination

Remember when you were a child, and your parents told you to eat the food you liked the least first so that you could enjoy the meal? There were always a few times you didn't do it, and you found yourself sitting at the table staring at a pile of ice-cold peas while your mother told you there'd be no dessert until you finished them.

Most of life is the same way. There are things we want to do and experience, and things we don't.

For various reasons, procrastinators will, instead of doing things they find difficult, unpleasant, or distasteful, put them off until tomorrow, next week, or some other time in the future. Sometimes, they will eventually get done. Often because the consequences of not doing them would be too severe. But usually, they just never get done – like those challenging conversations or starting your exercise plan.

Procrastination usually starts with a genuine intention to get to the thing we don't want to do. Still, as time passes, it becomes less likely that it will be done well or at all.

This is the same for everyone, so don't beat yourself up if you're doing it. Let's figure out why.

Mental Triggers

Everybody procrastinates about various things for slightly different reasons, but all of those reasons are mental triggers. Most of the time, they're subconscious, in that we don't even realize that we're giving ourselves permission to put them off. Here's why we do that.

Fear of Failure

Many people who procrastinate are highly intelligent, accomplished, and successful. When they do things, they do it exceptionally well (which is often why procrastination doesn't completely destroy their studies or careers.)

The problem is, when you're used to succeeding and being the best at what you do, it is terrifying to imagine an outcome where you don't.

This is why so many people put things off. They aren't entirely sure that they can deliver the results others expect from them or that they expect from themselves. They're so used to succeeding (often effortlessly) that they choose not to try rather than risking failure.

After all, not doing something isn't the same as not doing it well, is it?

Fear of Success

The flip side of the same coin is the fear of success. We are often scared to grab hold of opportunities because if we succeed, things might change. Change is scary. We get used to the groove that we live in, and we don't want to venture too far from it.

Even though the idea of success and the change it might bring scares us, we also don't want to be seen as weak or unambitious.

So instead of going for the opportunity and taking the chance, or turning it down and moving on, we do nothing. If someone else decides for us, it's not our fault that it didn't happen, right?

When people are afraid of success, they may avoid things they feel could move them to the next level. This would force them to make tough choices and welcome change in their career, home life, or relationships.

Fear of Disappointing Others

Sometimes, it's not a fear of failure for our own sake that causes us to procrastinate. Sometimes it's a fear of what our failure might mean for other people.

Maybe you have a very successful parent who wants you to follow in their footsteps. Maybe your boss or professor has decided you are their protégé. Their opinion of you matters profoundly, and the thought of letting them down can be debilitating.

If you want to please someone else with your results, it can lead to procrastination. The closer you get to delivering the result, the sooner you will find out if you are good enough for them.

Victimhood

Sometimes, people procrastinate because they are hoping someone else will swoop in and rescue them.

This is very often the case when this has been your experience in life. If you have or had a parent, spouse, or someone else who routinely stepped or steps in to save you when you have left something too late, you might become used to being the "damsel in distress." If you're used to having a brave knight rescue you, you might never develop the personal responsibility necessary to commit.

The problem with an arrangement like this is that there are no guarantees that your hero will always be there, and when they aren't, you will be in considerably more trouble.

. . .

Perfectionism

Perfectionism is often seen as a virtue, and there's indeed nothing wrong with wanting to deliver only your best.

However, many perfectionists also experience crippling stress about delivering not only their best, but the best there is.

When faced with a task that they are not absolutely sure they can knock completely out of the park, perfectionists often choose avoidance instead. Again, if you never actually do it, you can't possibly get it wrong, can you?

Perfectionists know they will do a good job, but good is not good enough, and until they can figure out how to make it flawless, they might simply avoid the problem.

Self-Sabotage

Sometimes, people procrastinate and then deliberately fail or under-deliver because, deep down, they don't believe they deserve to succeed.

If you are sabotaging yourself, you may take on tasks or responsibilities with good intentions. Still, over time, without even knowing that you're doing it, you might be setting yourself up to fail.

Overwhelmed

Sometimes, even the most capable, smart, and dependable people just have too much on their plate, and they just can't cope. So, while they might say yes to something, they soon come to regret it and try to find ways to avoid the problem.

In most cases, these people would be perfectly capable of getting whatever it is done right. They just don't have the energy or the time to devote to doing it to the standard they expect from themselves or within the timeframe they have promised it by.

Unfortunately, most highly capable people don't realize that they have limits and are human too. Even if they might ordinarily be able to handle something, sometimes, life intercedes. It's much harder to deliver at work, for instance, when you're also dealing with a home crisis, or studies, or something else.

So, while you say yes without a second thought, you soon realize that you might have bitten off more than you can chew.

Laziness

Unfortunately, sometimes, procrastination is a result of nothing more than laziness.

Today, more than ever before, we're used to getting what we want without trying too hard. Everything is instant, and we never have to wait for anything.

If we get too used to instant gratification, anything that does require effort and hard work may be too much for us. We know that there are rewards to be had, but they're just not enough to justify the time and energy we need to put into the process to get them.

Boredom

Imagine if you had to watch your favorite movie every day for the rest of your life. Or eat your favorite food for every meal. If you're like most people, you would soon come to hate whatever that thing might be.

When you are bored, whether it's in your job, in your studies, your relationship, or even an activity you used to love to do but have grown out of love with, you might try to avoid it.

Since people will probably expect you to behave the same way you always have, you might accept the task or activity in question. Still, you try to avoid and ignore it, hoping it will go away before you get around to it.

Negative Self Talk

We all rely on our self-esteem to drive us through life. It's what pushes us to try new things, learn more, become better at what we do and build new relationships.

Unfortunately, for whatever reason, sometimes our self-esteem lets us down.

You might have taken something on with excitement and energy, but over time, that little voice in your head that tells you you're not good enough to get involved. As your confidence erodes, so does your desire to find out whether you're as capable as you first thought.

Of course, this is a self-perpetuating cycle because the more you fail or fail to even try, the less you will believe in your ability to deliver.

The Size of the Task

There's an old saying: How do you eat an elephant? One bite at a time.

Unfortunately, very few of us take a step back often enough to even realize that we're dealing with an elephant at all. We stand so close to it, staring at the sheer scale of the problem, that we can't even fully see what we're dealing with.

While it would be easy to break the huge, very daunting thing we're facing into small steps so we can gain momentum and build out confidence on the way, we waste our time trying to work out how to do it all in one "gulp."

Competition

Finally, if you're a very competitive person, you may hesitate and procrastinate on tasks where you could be compared to someone else, whether at work, at home, or at school.

We all like to win, but there are some people out there for whom winning is everything. If you're one of them, you have probably already experienced this. You know you can do a great job of something, but you don't want to try, just in case you're not the best.

The thing is, life isn't a competition. We're all going to be first sometimes, second sometimes, and not even make the podium at other times. If you only do things where you can win, you will be missing out on many of the great things about being alive!

Change Always Starts with Self Knowledge

There will always be things we want to change about ourselves. The good news is that there is usually a way to make that change or alter our behavior enough to get a better result.

You can never fundamentally change who you are as a person or your deepest values. But you can improve the things you don't like, or that don't advance your happiness.

Everything always starts with self-knowledge, though, so now that we have touched on some of the common reasons why people procrastinate, it's time to pause and consider your own experiences. *Why do you procrastinate? Which of these common reasons most reflect you?*

You might want to decide on your own, but it is often easier to ask people you love and trust too. They may be able to see things about you that you haven't even recognized.

Self-Reflection

When did you realize you were procrastinating?
Do you recognize procrastination habits that
were formed as you were a child, or did things
start later in life?

Which mental triggers play the most significant
role in your procrastination? One specifically or
a combination of several?

Fears:

Victimhood:

Perfectionism:

Self-sabotage:

Overwhelmed:

Laziness:

Boredom:

Negativity:

Size of task:

Competition:

PUTTING OFF AN EASY THING MAKES IT *HARD*, AND PUTTING OFF A HARD ONE MAKES IT *IMPOSSIBLE*.

- *George H. Lorimer*

THREE

Mental Gymnastics

We know that you probably started to procrastinate when you were a child or a teen. That you do it because there is an instant payoff, even though you're trading it for long-term stress, anxiety, and pain. We even know the more common reasons why you might unconsciously be making this choice.

But as they say, knowledge is power, but without action, power is useless.

Examining and understanding your reasons and motivations is a good start, but you still need to learn how to change those things. Habits are tough to break, and they take consistency and commitment.

Before we get to specific actions you can take to retrain yourself, it's time to look at the mental preparation you need to do to get ready to change.

Habits are, in a very real way, things we are addicted to. If you've ever tried to change an addiction, like for instance, smoking, you know that the act of quitting is one of the last steps. Not the first.

Long before you take a concrete step to break an addiction, you need to give yourself time to think it through. To talk yourself through the steps. To share your goals with the people who care about you and to enlist their help. So, before we get into action, let's look at the thought process.

It's All in Your Mind

Some habits, like smoking, have a physical and a mental component, but when it comes to habits like procrastination, it really is all in your mind.

At some point in the past, you talked yourself into putting things off, so the logical first step is to talk yourself into why you shouldn't do that anymore.

If you're reading this book, then you've had enough adverse effects from procrastination to want to make a change, so why not start by listing the things you are losing or missing out on because you are a procrastinator?

Writing things down makes them real, and then if you spend some time reading those things back to yourself whenever you get a chance, you will start to reinforce your reasons for wanting to change. Talking yourself into procrastination caused the problem, so talking yourself out of it is the start of the solution.

Make copies of your list if you need to and leave it in places where you will see it often. Above the coffee maker. On the bathroom mirror. On the edge of your monitor.

You don't have to do anything at this stage except start to reprogram the way you think.

Willpower and Changing Habits

A little while ago, I compared breaking the habit of procrastination with breaking the habit and addiction to smoking. That wasn't just an analogy. It's something I have lived, and it was the single greatest example of procrastination in my own life.

I started smoking when I was in my early teens. By the time I was in my mid to late twenties, I already wanted to stop, but I kept putting it off for many of the reasons I mentioned earlier in this book. I was scared I would fail. I was scared of how it would affect my personality. I was scared of letting go of a crutch that I used to cope. I was scared it was going to be difficult.

For many more years, I procrastinated about quitting smoking. I continued to risk my health and literally burn money.

Finally, I realized that even if I didn't believe I had the willpower, I was pretty sure I had the won't power. I convinced myself that all I had to do was say no to the NEXT cigarette, and then the next, and so on.

It's been years since I had a puff, and the only thing I regret is not doing it sooner. That's not to say that it was easy. But it was a lot easier than I had convinced myself it would be.

When it comes to willpower, we tend to grossly underestimate ourselves. We believe that we're a lot weaker than we actually are and that we're sure to fail because we're not strong enough.

We also convince ourselves that this is an all-or-nothing equation. That we have to beat our habits on the first attempt, or it will be impossible to break them at all.

Neither of those things are true.

Willpower is not always easy to muster, and it's not always consistent. There will always be times when we slip up and go back to our old ways for a little while. That's understandable. They've been our normal for a long time, and normal is comfortable.

But the real trick to willpower is not to let one setback derail our goals. When you find yourself sliding back into an unwanted habit like procrastinating, you don't have to throw in the towel and decide you have failed. In fact, what you do need to do is double down, work harder, and trust that you're in control.

Even if it doesn't always feel like it, you are always in control of your choices and what you do, and you can choose not to give up. That's true willpower.

A Word About Mental Health

We're already pretty far into this book, and we've covered a lot of the thought processes and mental blocks that may be standing between you and beating procrastination.

It's a great thing to be on a journey of self-discovery and to take charge of our thoughts, beliefs, and actions.

We can all achieve amazing things when we have the right mindset and when we apply our minds to problems, including this one. However, self-help, willpower, and mindset are never a replacement for professional help when it comes to mental health.

If the reasons you are experiencing any of the common triggers for procrastination are due to past, unresolved trauma, or if you believe that anxiety, depression, or any other mental health condition are the root cause of your problem, you should always seek professional counseling or therapy.

A book like this can still help you to address the specific steps necessary to beat procrastination. Still, it can't solve the underlying causes of the problem. Those causes may be manifesting in other areas of your life and may lead to other, more serious issues.

You wouldn't start training for a marathon with a broken leg, so don't try to fix problems like this without getting also paying attention to any more significant issues you might have.

The Power of Starting

Hopefully by now, you see that it is possible to break the habit of procrastination, even if it's been with you for years or decades. It's possible to break any bad habit, at any time of your life, if you want to badly enough.

That's a pretty inspiring realization, and if you are ready to make the change, it will give you the boost you need to get started and the momentum to keep going. That's great. You're going to need it!

If you aren't already excited to get started, then you're probably not ready yet. Spend some more time examining your reasons, figuring out why you have been procrastinating, and building up that reservoir of willpower. (Or won't power. Stubbornness is a great motivator!)

When you have everything straight in your own mind, start telling people you love, trust, and respect what you plan to do and when you plan to start.

There's a reason we call the people in our lives our "support system." When we're going through or tackling something difficult, they're the people that help to keep us focused and remind us why we're doing it at all. They're the people that will hold us accountable and help us up when we stumble.

You can make life changes like beating procrastination on your own, but it's likely to be a lot harder than it had to be.

Before we move on to actionable steps you can take, there's one more thing you need to know.

Quitting anything, beating any bad habit, and any kind of major personal transformation is a marathon, not a sprint.

The momentum you get from being excited to start will carry you forward for a while. Your support system will be a big help along the way, but there will come a time when you feel like you have run out of steam. When it feels like you should just give up, accept yourself with your flaws, and live with the consequences.

Hopefully, by the time you reach that point, you will already have implemented strategies to keep you on track and turn those into new habits.

Regardless, however, you need to remember that nothing worth doing is ever easy. Even if you slip. Even if you can't win every battle, it's important never to give up. You only fail if you quit.

Self-Reflection

What is your procrastination costing you?

What are some things you enjoy and want to
start? What do you want to accomplish?

Self-Reflection

What are the main obstacles you face that are preventing you from starting something you want to achieve?

IT IS NOT
BECAUSE THINGS
ARE DIFFICULT
THAT WE DO NOT
DARE, IT IS
BECAUSE WE DO
NOT DARE THAT
THEY ARE
DIFFICULT.

- Seneca

Strategies to Deal With Procrastination

Everything we do in life begins in our minds. First, we have the idea. Then we refine the idea. Then we come up with a plan, and we spend some time psyching ourselves up to execute.

But, like everything in life, the time to execute always comes a little bit sooner than we expect. Since we're trying to beat procrastination, execution is possibly the most critical when you have gone through all those other steps.

It can be scary to think about changing how you interact with the world. Still, if you've worked through the mental preparation steps by now, you should be mostly ready to get started.

It's important to note there that I said mostly.

Nothing in life will ever be completely perfect. There will never be one moment where everything is exactly right.

Close enough is good enough. So, if you've been waiting for the perfect moment, don't. It's probably just another way you're allowing yourself to put this off.

Growth is not easy. Sometimes, you just have to take the first step and trust the process.

FOUR

Steps Towards Productivity

"The journey of a thousand miles begins with one step." Lao Tzu

And now, we get to the true test of the procrastinator's mettle: taking action.

If you really are a true, dyed in the wool procrastinator, just making it this far is a huge deal. It's a good time to stop, take a deep breath, and pat yourself on the back.

Then, it's time to get to work.

One of the common issues for procrastinators is the magnitude of the task at hand. It's a common thread throughout most of the reasons we procrastinate, so everything in this chapter is divided into smaller, bite-sized chunks that are a lot less daunting to tackle.

That in itself is one of the best strategies out there and worth remembering. Nearly everything can be broken down into smaller tasks, and when you do that, they seem a lot more attainable.

I should also mention that most of the steps in this part of the book will look simple and easy to achieve, but actually doing them, and more importantly, doing them *consistently*, can be challenging. Again, take it in small, manageable steps. Don't expect to change a lifetime's worth of habits overnight. It will take time. Give yourself plenty of leeway to build new, better habits. Enjoy the list of strategies below, and try out what would work best for you.

Find Your Weaknesses

The first thing you need to do to start beating procrastination is to figure out what your specific weaknesses are.

Even people who are masters at putting things off won't do it with everything. There is almost certainly a long list of things that you never struggle with, but also a list of things you do.

Before you start taking any other actions, think about the last ten things you struggle to start and finish, and then consider what they have in common.

Do you try to avoid things that you don't enjoy doing? Do you put off things that might require confrontation of some kind? Are there some tasks that bore you?

Some people tend to put off mundane, ordinary, or tedious everyday tasks in favor of new and exciting projects. Some might avoid activities or projects that require them to work with a particular person or technology.

If there are specific reasons like this to work on, you should tackle them first. Consider new technologies that might help to speed up the boring tasks you don't enjoy. Communicate problems you may have working with a particular person and so on. These are "structural" problems that may be easier to solve than the other things on your list, and when you're trying to make significant life changes, even small victories can give you a big boost!

Visual Cues

The next step I'd recommend in the process of beating procrastination is developing a system of visual cues for yourself.

Many people who procrastinate tend to put the things they are avoiding on the bottom shelf or in a special email folder. Out of sight is out of mind, and if you don't see it, you won't be constantly reminded to get it done.

Seeing the things that we are avoiding is uncomfortable, and in this case, discomfort might be a good thing. Being reminded of what you need to get done will motivate you to get it done, just so that you don't have to see it anymore.

While there are several strategies to do this, one of the best, simplest, and most cost-effective is to have a whiteboard somewhere where you list all your important to-do list items. When the task is always there, you can't ignore it or pretend it doesn't exist, and eventually, you will have to tackle it just to get rid of it.

This is a quick and easy method to hold yourself personally accountable, and that's a great way to make sure things get done!

Pause Before Saying Yes

Not everyone procrastinates because they have too much to do, but it's not uncommon.

Many of us are so used to agreeing to everything people ask us to do that we don't even stop to think before we say yes.

This means that we end up with all sorts of tasks on our list that we really don't want to do, don't have time to do, or shouldn't be doing at all. Once you've committed to it, it's on your list, but it's really not surprising that you procrastinate because you didn't want to do it in the first place.

Agreeing to things before we have the time to consider whether we have time, energy, or inclination only creates unnecessary stress and anxiety. If you're already struggling with procrastination in general, that only compounds the situation.

The next thing you should do to thin your to-do list and reduce the vicious cycle you may be finding yourself in is to pause and think before you say yes to anything.

Instead of automatically saying yes to anything your boss, friends, spouse, parent, or child asks you to do for them, ask them if you can get back to them. Then consider whether you really want to do it, have the time, and have the necessary skills and tools needed to get it done.

Once you have done that, you have a few options: you can accept the task, you can accept but ask for modifications or assistance, or you can decline. That's very important. With the exception of projects for work and assignments for school or college, you often have the option to say no.

If you believe that accepting a task or request will cause you stress or anxiety, or that you will procrastinate because you don't want to do it or just can't, say no. It's allowed!

Manage Expectations

If your procrastination is related to fear of failure, and in particular, how your failure might affect someone else, the next important thing you need to do is to manage the expectations of others.

If you are taking on a new project at work or doing something that you have never done before, it's okay to say that while you will do your best, you will need feedback and assistance. All but the most unreasonable managers and employers will understand that if it's the first time you're taking on this type of magnitude of a project, you might not nail it completely on the first try and need some help.

Instead of pretending that you're 100% certain you'll completely kill it, voice your concerns, but assure them that you will do your best, as always. If you're not absolutely terrified not to meet overly high expectations all on your own, you'll be much less likely to avoid the project altogether.

If you procrastinate because you're afraid to disappoint a loved one or parent, managing expectations is important too.

We often try to avoid doing things that we're not sure we can excel at because we're afraid we won't measure up. When you know that the only standards you need to meet are the ones you set for yourself, you'll be far more likely to start, finish, and even be excited about the process.

Whether you're dealing with employers, relatives, spouses, or customers, it's always a good idea to under-promise and over-deliver. If you're not setting the bar unreasonably high for yourself, you'll be a lot more relaxed and much more motivated.

Just Start

Many people procrastinate because a job seems too big, too technical, or too hard. They have no idea where to start, so they just don't start at all.

Of course, deadlines always arrive, and even the things we're scared of still have to get done. So, ignoring the elephant in the room is not a successful strategy.

The best advice here is to throw caution to the wind and just get started.

Dive right in. Read the instructions. Figure out the problem. Ask people questions. Make notes. Wrap your head around things and make notes about how you can best tackle the project.

Even five, ten, or thirty minutes of really getting into something you're afraid to start can demystify the problem, help you develop a strategy, and take it out of the "avoid" pile.

Do Boring Things First

Many people who procrastinate aren't afraid or anxious about the things they avoid. They're just bored and hate doing them.

Maybe you're a creative person who hates doing accounting tasks, so you leave them to pile up until they're an unmanageable mountain. Perhaps you really find doing the laundry mind-numbing, so you leave it until it takes over your home.

Avoiding boring tasks will never make them go away, and because boring tasks tend to be the day-to-day things that keep everything running, if you keep avoiding them, you'll only be faced with a massive amount of them when you finally get around to them.

Spend a little time at the start of every day getting the things you don't enjoy done, so you can focus on the things you love for the rest of the day.

Reward Yourself

A writer I follow online talks about "candy bar scenes," which are the scenes she is really looking forward to writing.

What most people don't know about writing is that it's an arduous, difficult process much of the time. You might think it sounds easy to make up stories, but when you're faced with the prospect of a blank screen and tens of thousands of words to weave out of thin air, it's anything but. In fact, it's often much easier to spend an hour on social media and bathe the cat than it is to summon the muse.

The writer I mentioned forces herself to write a fixed number of words and then allows herself a "candy bar scene" as a reward.

Find ways to reward yourself for tackling the tasks you're avoiding. Whether it's a walk in a park at lunch or a cup of coffee when you get it done. If you have an incentive to get the work done, you'll be far more likely to do it.

Change the Scenery

Sometimes, the reason we aren't productive isn't because of a particular task or project. It's simply because we are in a rut. We humans are creative creatures. We need to be inspired, motivated, and challenged.

If you're finding it hard to start or finish something in your office or in the place you usually work, go somewhere else.

If you've ever come up with the answer to a particularly challenging problem in a strange place, like brushing your teeth or walking your dog, you know just how valuable it can be to think about and tackle problems in unexpected settings.

Many people like to work in places like coffee shops rather than their office because the buzz, noise, and activity helps trigger inspiration.

Another way to "change the scenery" is to discuss the problem with someone you trust. Even if they don't know exactly how the project or task works, it can be invaluable to bounce ideas off someone. Sometimes, they will have an idea that might trigger a solution, but sometimes, they just help you organize your thoughts.

Timing Is Important

As I've already said, it's usually best to "eat the broccoli" or do the tedious and unpleasant tasks first. Still, there are other ways timing can help you to stay on track.

If you have a very complex task to tackle, it might not be a good idea to work on it late in the afternoon, when you're already tired. Try to schedule tasks that require a lot of muscle or brainpower for times when you're up to the challenge.

Likewise, many people are frazzled and a little grumpy on Monday mornings, which doesn't equate to the best conditions to tackle collaborative tasks. Timing plays a huge role. There are optimal times for most of the tasks you need to accomplish, and if you schedule them accordingly, you will have a much easier time getting them done.

The other important timing issue to consider is YOUR personal body clock. Some of us are morning people. Some of us are night owls. You know yourself and your habits best, so build your schedule around your own preferences.

Record Your "Wins"

There's a reason so many people love to keep an actual to-do list.

There are very few things in life as satisfying as crossing actual tasks off of a real list. Lists not only help remind you what needs to get done, but they also give you the opportunity to see a visual record of your progress. Success breeds success, after all!

If you really want to hack the to-do list, break projects down into individual tasks, and list absolutely everything you have to do, from calling HR to lunch with a client. There's nothing more motivational than looking at your to-do list and seeing exactly how productive you actually are.

It might surprise you to learn this, but there's actual science involved here.

When we accomplish tasks (and cross them off our list!), our brains release a neurotransmitter known as dopamine. This natural chemical gives us a feeling of happiness, satisfaction, and accomplishment. So, there's a bona fide biological reason why we feel good when we get stuff done.

Even better, when you're feeling great from dopamine, it gets easier to tackle tasks that you might not be looking forward to.

Time Chunking

Even if you've never heard of time chunking or the Pomodoro technique, chances are, you used it when you studied for a test. In fact, this has been a proven and popular way to improve productivity since the 1980s, and it's still a top management tool.

Many studies over the years have shown that human beings study and work best in short, intense bursts, interspersed with short breaks. So instead of trying to force yourself to focus for hours, set a timer, work like crazy until it goes off, and then walk away for a few minutes.

Clear your head, take a walk, speak to a colleague, have a coffee, and then go back to the task you were working on. It may seem counterintuitive, but this is one of the best ways to stay focused, keep your brain sharp and alert, and improve time management.

Create Tasks and Milestones

If you've ever seen a project manager at work, you will know that there are seemingly infinite steps along the way between A and Z on their project plans.

That's because project managers know that it's easiest to get things done, measure progress, and solve problems along the way if they're only dealing with small parts of the whole at any one time.

Of course, they are usually dealing with several team members who are doing different parts of the project simultaneously, but you can still borrow the technique. Here's how it works:

- Think about the significant steps that need to be accomplished along the way to completing the project or task you are working on. These will be your milestones.
- Now consider each milestone as its own mini-

project and further break it down into tinier activities and goals. These will be your tasks.

- Tasks and milestones can be carried out in sequence or in any order you like (although it's usually easier to have them in some sort of chronological order!)
- Keep track of the milestones and tasks on the list.

Project managers often use complicated software to track tasks and milestones, which lets them assign time and resources to each one. While you don't have to do that, it is very motivating to keep track of what you have completed and what's still to be done. Again, having a visual record of what you've already achieved is a great motivator and will help you keep the momentum going.

Set Deadlines

If you don't have a firm deadline for a project or task, it can be easy to put it off.

The truth is, everything eventually comes due, and the longer it's been since it landed on your "plate," the closer you are to being asked for it.

If you've ever hidden something away in the *"bottom drawer"* that you're trying to ignore, you have probably already experienced that as more time passes, you become more and more anxious.

An excellent way to avoid this is to set your own deadlines. Even if there's an external deadline for something, it's a good idea to set your own deadline for a few days before it is needed. That way, you'll have enough time to double-check and polish everything.

Deadlines are just another way to hold ourselves account-able, and accountability is crucial in preventing and curbing procrastination.

Ditch Distractions

There's not a person out there today (at least, not one who is likely to be reading this) that isn't bombarded with dozens of distractions every hour. Social media notifica-tions. Text messages. Video chats. Breaking news! It's all around us, all the time.

Many authors have a technology-driven trick – software that prevents them from doing anything but using a word processor for a predetermined period of time.

While you don't need special software, it's a good idea to close your social media if it's usually open while you are working on something. Put your phone away, and if you can, disconnect from the internet. With so many things demanding our attention, it's very easy to get distracted by shiny things, and before you know it, half your day is gone!

Start Small

Not everyone procrastinates about everything.

Some of us are utterly capable productivity machines in our jobs or studies but procrastinate about life or relation-ship decisions. We can be very comfortable at work or school but find it hard to tackle more personal issues.

Whether it's work, health, or relationships, though, if you put things off for too long, you're going to be inviting even more trouble than you were trying to avoid.

If you tend to procrastinate in one area of your life but are fine with other things, it might just be the sheer size of the change that could come from a particular action that is putting you off.

Maybe you're procrastinating about striking out on your own and launching your business because you're not sure you can succeed. Don't try to do it all in one big chunk! Find a more minor, sideline version that you can start in your downtime to test the waters.

Maybe you're hesitating to make a change in a personal relationship. Start small, with one conversation or a single change.

Want to write a book, but aren't sure how to start, so you've never actually tried? Spend some time writing an outline of chapters and scenes. Even if it takes a month to get it done, you will feel a lot more confident when you're done.

Life doesn't always have to be about leaping into the unknown. It's okay to dip a toe in first!

Be Task Driven

When I was a lot younger, I used to do a lot of walking. Not always by choice! Particularly as a student, I spent a lot of time trudging from college to transit and back again.

When I had long distances to walk, one of my tricks was simply to put my head down, forget about the distance, and just concentrate on putting one foot down in front of the other. (*Stay alert and watch for poles and other obstacles when your head is down)*

When you ignore the seemingly impossibly long distance (*or difficult task*) in its entirety and just focus on getting the next task done, it becomes a lot less daunting. When you're not panicking about the whole project, it's a lot easier to stay focused, and when you do, you will be surprised how much you get done.

Back when I used to walk long distances, I often found that when I did look up, I was a lot closer to the goal than I thought I would be. The whole walk certainly seemed easier and even faster.

Don't Use Procrastination as a Crutch

Very often, we use our weaknesses as a bit of a crutch. We will warn people jokingly that we are terrible procrastinators, but what we're really doing is setting them up to be less disappointed when we don't complete something on time or at all.

You can have the tendency to procrastinate without letting it become the norm in your life, but you have to admit that it's a problem. You also have to be determined not to let it take over.

Perfectionists can learn to let little things go. Stress junkies can learn to relax. People take anger management classes to get their emotions under control. Procrastination is just another personal trait that you can conquer.

Make A Decision - Any Decision

Very often, people will procrastinate about decisions. They will put them off until someone else makes them or until there is no longer a decision to be made. If someone else makes it for you or it becomes a moot point, you're off the hook, aren't you?

The truth is, decision-making is terrifying for a lot of people. We'd rather lose an opportunity than choose the wrong thing, but that's the wrong attitude to have.

Firstly, not making a decision is a decision in itself, and it will almost always not go the way you would have hoped it would.

Secondly, if you make the wrong choice, you can usually change things afterward, but there may not be any second chance if you do nothing.

People are often scared that if they make the wrong choices, someone will be angry, upset, or annoyed with us, but the truth is, they'd still be those things if you do nothing. In fact, if you do nothing, you have a 100% chance of upsetting everyone. But if you do something, you have at least a 50% chance you'll get it right!

Always in the Driver's Seat

Hopefully, these practical techniques you can use to get your tendency to procrastinate under control help change the way you think. Remember, though, procrastination is a habit, and it takes a long time to break a habit.

Every time you use one of these strategies, it is a small victory. Still, you will need to consciously choose to use them every time you feel yourself slipping back into your old habits.

Procrastination is just another way we try to evade personal responsibility. If we don't do something, we can't get it wrong, and that's an attractive proposition in many ways. But it's not one that will get you where you want to go.

Try to remember that in your life, you're always in the driver's seat. You always make the choices, and you always decide what you do or don't do. It's scary to think that way, but it's also empowering once you get used to it.

You CAN change your habits. YOU can get things done. It's all in your hands, and if you take action and get something wrong, you can always try something else!

Now that you know how to get started, let's find out more about how you can keep going.

Self-Reflection

What 5 strategies mentioned throughout the chapter could fit best to you and make the most significant impact?

Self-Reflection

How could you implement these 5 strategies
in your day-to-day life?

**DON'T PUT OFF
FOR TOMORROW
WHAT YOU CAN
DO TODAY
BECAUSE IF YOU
ENJOY IT TODAY,
YOU CAN DO IT
AGAIN
TOMORROW.**

- James A. Michener

Maintenance

PART 3

There's a saying about addictions: falling off the wagon. Even years after someone has beaten an addiction, they can slip up and fall back into their own ways.

While procrastination isn't exactly an addiction, it is a habit, and that's very similar, as we've already discussed. So even if you are using all those new tools to get things done and checked off the list, there's always a chance that you might slide back.

This section of the book helps us look at how to stay on track with your new tools and what to do if you don't.

FIVE

Creating New Habits

"Depending on what they are, our habits will either make us or break us. We become what we repeatedly do."
—*Sean Covey*

Sean Covey knows a thing or two about habits. After all, he's written several mega-bestselling books about them. So, it's a good idea to take his advice to heart!

You've probably spent a lifetime building up bad habits, so it's unlikely you will break them overnight, or even in a week or a month. But if you can repeat the tips this book outlines, you can break those negative habits and keep them broken.

Have you ever had the experience where you've driven somewhere familiar, and when you get there, you don't remember the trip? You were completely awake and drove without incident. Still, nothing remarkable happened, so the journey itself is a bit of a blur? After many years of driving, it becomes a habit. We do things automatically, without thinking. When we're also following a familiar route, there's nothing to trigger any specific memory of the drive.

That's what habits are like. When you start building them, you have to really concentrate – like a learner driver. But over time, we get so used to doing things in a specific way, it becomes automatic, and we do it without thinking. That's the power of repetition. You will get there. But for now, here's what you can do to keep yourself on track.

Staying on Track

Building habits takes time and repetition. You're going to have to do things the same way over and over before they become "your way of doing things."

The good news is people break habits and make new ones all the time.

The bad news is that there's no fixed end date. No one can tell you it will take x amount of times or a certain number of weeks or months. You're going to have to keep pushing yourself to act a little out of character until it stops feeling uncomfortable and just becomes the way you do things.

If you're someone who puts off difficult conversations, avoids following dreams, or puts complex tasks at the bottom of the tray, it's going to be hard at the beginning. But it will become easier over time, guaranteed.

It's Okay to Fail

One of the worst things we collectively believe, is that failure is the end.

We're so scared to fail at anything that we very often talk ourselves out of trying at all. Ironically, that's also one of the big reasons why we procrastinate in the first place.

But failure is not the end, and it's not always bad. In fact, many of the most successful people in the world failed often, and sometimes spectacularly, before they had their big successes.

The same is true of making changes in your life and your habits.

You will almost certainly fail. You will almost certainly slide back into your old ways once or twice. Especially when life gets tough and it feels comfortable. The trick is not to take one slip as the end of the road.

You won't always come first or be the best, but that is perfectly okay. It's okay not to be the best at everything you do. It's okay to acknowledge that you procrastinate out of fear and that you're actually putting off dealing with that because you're scared too.

Learning to do anything new is a process, and changing your own bad habits is nothing different. It will take time to make changes stick, so take it easy on yourself.

Instead of beating yourself up when you catch yourself putting something off, try to learn what your triggers are. It might not make them easier to avoid, but it will help you to see them coming!

Set Rules for Yourself

Not everybody procrastinates about everything. Some people do it at work. Some people do it at home. Some put off making health changes. Some avoid tough conversations. Whatever it is, you're going to start seeing patterns.

When you do, it might help to make concessions.

For instance, if you procrastinate at work or school, you might give yourself permission to avoid starting challenging projects on a Friday. But when Monday rolls around, make sure it's at the very top of the to-do list so you don't make a habit of putting it off.

If you're procrastinating about going to the gym, try getting yourself to go every second day or to skip one session per week.

Whatever rules you set for yourself, you need to stick to, but you also need to give yourself a break sometimes. Do you remember rebelling against teachers and parents when you were a child, and they made too many rules? That little kid is still there, and they will rebel against you as well!

You will gain a lot more by setting reasonable limits and allowing yourself some leeway than you will by beating yourself up every time you're not absolutely perfect.

One Thing at a Time

Changing your life is great. Building new habits is admirable. But it's also not something you can do in a week. Or when you have a ton of other things going on in your life.

Be honest with yourself. Do you really have time right now to start an ambitious diet and exercise plan, or would it be better to start slow and build steadily to your goals? Sometimes biting off more than you can chew will actually set you back further. It also leaves you feeling despondent when you don't get superhuman results.

Likewise, if you're going through major upheavals in your life, like a new job, new relationship, health concerns, or serious personal issues, it may not be the best time to try mastering your procrastination. Yes, you might want to feel empowered, but if you have so much on your plate already, it could be better to spend that energy elsewhere.

The best way to tackle a problem like this is by setting yourself up for success. That's not to say that you should find excuses to put it off, but you also need to be realistic.

Make Incremental Changes

Whatever it is that you have been putting off, and however determined you are to finally get a handle on it, you have to know that your first plan probably won't work exactly as you intend.

You probably won't find the magic formula on the first go, and you'll almost certainly find that some of the ideas and tips in this book won't work for you. That's okay. It's okay to make changes to your original plan as you go along. It's even okay to change your goals slightly.

So, maybe you won't get fit enough to run the Boston Marathon. But you can almost certainly get fit enough to do well in your local park run.

Maybe you can't take on that high-profile project at work all on your own. But you can probably be a great team leader and collaborate with a whole lot of talented people.

As you move towards your goals, take note of what works,

and do more of that. Pay attention to what doesn't work too, and try to do it a little differently, or find a new idea altogether. Changing your mind as you improve yourself is not only acceptable but also expected!

Lean on Your Support System

You've probably heard the saying "it takes a village" way too many times in your life.

But when it comes to making significant changes in your life, it's more than just a modern-day cliché.

Sharing your goal to be more accountable and stop putting things off with people you know, love, and trust is a great way to make sure you stay on task. Particularly if they are people who will hold you accountable when you try to let yourself off the hook.

You don't have to tell everyone about your mission to change your ways, but the ones you do share that information with can help a lot. Some might be gentler and remind you quietly of your goals. Others might forcefully remove you from bed to go on that jog you promised you would. They're all valuable parts of your team.

You Got This

Trying to change yourself is, without a doubt, one of the hardest things you will ever do.

Without someone directly telling you what to do,

measuring results, and ensuring you stay on track, you're probably going to feel a little overwhelmed. There will be times when you want to give up and when you're convinced you will never get the results you want.

That's okay. That's normal.

Everyone has moments of self-doubt. But look at everything you've already done!

Just deciding to improve yourself and work on issues that aren't working for you is a huge, brave step. One that many people will never make. Remember that you don't have to be perfect. You're already great. You're already successful in so many ways.

Patience. The Other "P" Word

Isn't it funny that even if we're the biggest procrastinators out there, we expect other things to happen immediately? If you find yourself frustrated that you're not the, take charge productivity machine you dream of in a week, remember that.

When it comes to making lasting changes to your personality, and your life, slow and steady really does win the race. Focus on the end goal, don't let small slips phase you, and remember that if you aim for the moon, even if you miss, you still land among the stars. So even if you can't change every bad habit you have, you can always, *always* improve yourself!

Self-Reflection

What will make it most challenging to stay
on track?

What are some rules you can implement to
keep you going?
Examples - *no skipping 2 workouts in a row.
Write a 1000 word blog post at least once a week.*

OFTEN JUST BY TAKING ACTION, BY DOING SOMETHING ABOUT THE SITUATION CAN *RELIEVE* THE STRESS AND HELP *CORRECT* THE SITUATION.

- *Catherine Pulsifer*

SIX

Progress

Benjamin Franklin (who got a whole lot of stuff done in his own life!) once said, "If you fail to plan, you are planning to fail."

Planning, making checklists, and using tools like boards and charts might not seem like the sexiest thing in the world (and okay, they're not), but results are.

There's a reason we work harder for bosses that recognize our achievements, and there's a reason why star charts work for kids in school. We like it when people take note of the things we do well, and we like to be rewarded for them.

Here's the good news, though: you don't need someone else to do that for you! You can use planning and progress measuring tools yourself, and when you reach important milestones and goals along the way, you can absolutely reward yourself for doing a great job. In fact, if you do, you're likely to meet those milestones even faster!

In the Beginning: The Plan

The critical thing to remember about any plan is that it's not supposed to be written in stone. Even people who plan things for a living treat their plans and schedules as living documents. They update and modify as they progress, getting rid of things that don't work and adding more of the things that do.

If you're a dyed in the wool, lifelong procrastinator driven by a fear of making decisions and being wrong, or by fear of failure, you might find that you want to put this part off too. Don't.

No one ever gets a plan entirely right on the first try. It's more important than to make one (even if most of it changes later) than to make it perfect. Here's what you need to do:

- Write down your goal. Be as specific as possible. For instance, "complete X project by Y date," or "call back all my clients within 1 week," or "start my diet on X date." The more specific, the more accountable you will be.
- Now, write down steps you think you can take to start making that happen. Again, be specific, and if possible, add dates, times, and deliverables to each one.
- Set regular dates to review your progress. You will measure it against the details you've outlined above.

You don't have to immediately put your plan into action, but you should set a hard start date. Procrastinators will usually try to push things that don't have fixed start dates and deadlines back as much as possible, so make sure you set one and stick to it.

It doesn't matter how you make your plan either. You can write it in a book, use a computer, put it on a whiteboard or something else. Just get it down in writing because when we write things down, they instantly become more real.

Know Where You Started

There's a time management strategy known as S.M.A.R.T. goals, which are goals that are appropriately named Specific, Measurable, Achievable, Relevant, and Time-bound.

You will already have got most of that down in your plan by being specific, breaking things into manageable chunks, sticking to things that bring you closer to your goal, and setting deadlines and start dates.

But for your goals to be measurable, you will need to know where you are right now.

Again, take the time to write down how you feel about your situation right now. Whether that's swamped at work, failing a course, not fitting into your clothes, or something else. This part is challenging because it's hard to be brutally honest, even with yourself, but it's crucial.

When you review your progress in a week, a month, or a year, you're going to look at that piece of paper and be amazed at how far you've come, so let it all out!

Review and Audit

In order to know if your plan is working, you need to check in with yourself and really take note of what's going well and where you need to tweak your plan or work harder.

Again, because we procrastinators tend to put things off if we can, you need to treat this like an important meeting. Set aside a time every week and month when you can spend half an hour considering your progress and where you might have been less successful. It doesn't have to be a long time. Half an hour is usually more than enough.

Go over each part of your plan and the goals you have set for yourself, and rate how well you think you've done.

If you have specific steps, checklists, and milestones in your plan, consider whether you exceeded them, met them, or fell short. Now ask yourself why and what you can do better next time.

Remember that if you're consistently not meeting one type of goal or milestone, you might need to make changes to your plan.

We can change our personalities and our lives, but we also need to work with our nature. So, for instance, if your weight loss plan involves getting up at 5am to cycle on the stationary bike, but you're not a morning person, change the schedule! There's no rule that says you MUST do your cycling at the crack of dawn!

Changing our lives, personalities, and behavior is about training ourselves to do things differently and ALSO recognizing that we're individuals. What works for someone else might not work for you, and if you would do better and achieve more by doing it another way, that's okay too!

Make changes to your plan. Update tasks and milestones, and again, make sure you write everything down, so you can see your goals, progress, and achievements.

Celebrate Your Wins!

Have you ever trained a puppy? Notice how the easiest way to get them to sit, stay, or heel is with a treat? We're not very different from puppies.

Humans work best when we're rewarded for our hard work, and there's no one better than you to do that! Along with goals, milestones, tasks, and progress tracking, make sure you work rewards and celebrations into your plan.

Finished a giant project at work ahead of schedule? Take yourself out for dinner to celebrate!

Reached a milestone in your goal to get healthier? Buy yourself a new outfit that shows off your progress and makes you feel great.

Whatever it is that you have achieved, give yourself an appropriate reward for your hard work. Even if it's a quiet night at home watching your favorite movie. If that's what makes you feel good, do it.

Also, remember that you don't have to keep the rewards for the end of the process. You've got all those milestones and reviews built into your plan, so take those as an opportunity to reward progress too. Not only will this help to keep you motivated to get to the next big milestone, but it will also help to keep you going when you feel like things aren't working.

You also don't have to reward yourself only when you've come first, beaten all the other competition, or broken a record. You aren't competing against the rest of the world.

You're working to improve yourself. To grow, become more productive and to meet and exceed your own goals and records.

Stop comparing yourself to everyone else; they've got their own mountains to climb. You have nothing to prove to anyone but yourself.

Being Organized Works

You may have noticed a theme in this chapter. It's all about organizing your thoughts and goals, breaking them into chunks, and writing them down.

The reason for this is simple: being organized ahead of time will help you achieve your goals.

When we leave things up to chance, we give ourselves all sorts of opportunities to change our minds, back out of commitments, or put things off. But when we already know ahead of time what needs to happen, when, and why, there's no excuse not to get it done.

If you don't even have to think of your next step, and you just have to follow the plan, you're far more likely to do that – even when you don't want to. After all, even when you're having a bad day, it's tough to justify not doing it if you know exactly what you should be doing.

Don't be too rigid or unforgiving, though. There are times when we just can't get something done. When you get sick, have a family emergency, or something else. Get through whatever it is, then go back to the plan and just move things forward accordingly.

Your work or living space matters too. Many people who struggle with procrastination also struggle to stay organized. Still, if your space is in order, everything has a place and is in it, it's so much easier to put your hands on exactly what you need, exactly when you need it.

If your desk, office, or home is more chaotic and less organized, you might want to spend some time getting that all into shape too.

Self-Reflection

Know where you are starting from. How do
you picture your progress in a ...

Week?

Month?

Year?

Self-Reflection

In what ways can you "celebrate your wins"?

YOUR MIND IS FOR *HAVING* IDEAS, NOT *HOLDING* THEM.

- David Allen

Bonus

PART 4: MORE STRATEGIES & TOOLS

As procrastinators, we are hard-wired to prioritize our short-term "needs" over our long-term goals. Watching that show, playing a game, it all just provides a nice bit of instant gratification.

The strategies, along with the maintenance techniques laid out throughout the book, will help you conquer this annoying and stressful habit.

Still, this is not a problem that suddenly disappears overnight. If you are prone to put things off when they're uncomfortable or difficult, you've probably been doing it for years. Maybe even your whole life.

This is why nearly everything you're going to do now is going to be repetitive, carefully planned, with built-in accountability and measurable goals. You're going to take away some of that wiggle room so that you can stay focused and get things done.

But once you do, you're going to discover that you can do a whole lot more than you thought you could, and the fears and worries that are holding you back aren't really true at all. Eventually, you're going to learn to love that feeling of crossing things off the list, and you will become a productivity machine.

And until you do, you're going to fake it till you make it. This bonus section includes a few easy ways to build routine and accountability into your life. It will also cover how some apps, tools, and technology can actually help you be more productive. These thing's won't keep you endlessly scrolling down a feed but rather keep you focused and can relieve you from the anxieties of procrastinating.

SEVEN

O O O

Just In Case You Need More

"I have learned that champions aren't just born; champions can be made when they embrace and commit to life-changing positive habits." —*Lewis Howes*

No one is born successful, or accomplished, or productive. We are all a product of the things we repeatedly do, and any habits you don't like can be broken. You can change yourself, take control of your life, and become the person you want to be.

Every decision and choice you make will help, but sometimes, you need a little help getting used to making good choices. So, this chapter is about small, simple things you can start doing before you even try to tackle the big, scary ones.

They may not seem like much, but the more positive changes you can make, even the tiny ones, the closer you are to the you, you want to be.

Get Your Routine Ready for Change

Humans are creatures of habit, but even more than that, we're biologically programmed to need routines. Our bodies have built-in clocks, known as circadian rhythms, that literally dictate when we want to be awake and when we want to sleep.

Some people might be night owls while others are morning people, but it's a proven fact that light and dark directly impact those cycles. It's why we want to sleep more in the winter, when it's dark, and why we're more active in the summer!

If you learn to work with those rhythms, you'll get more done in the day, without even trying!

As much as we would all like to think that being impulsive and spontaneous drives creativity and helps us get things done, that's just not true. Even creative people get more done when they work according to a routine.

Plan your days to include all the important things you need to get done. Get up at roughly the same time every day (yes, even on weekends, although an extra hour or so won't be too bad for your routine!)

Make sure you eat breakfast before you start your day too. Low blood sugar makes us sluggish and less likely to get things done. If you drink coffee or tea, a cup to start the morning is another good idea.

Try to divide your day into blocks too, and consider how you feel at different times of the day. Many people sense that by late afternoon, they are tired and find it hard to concentrate, so that's not the best time to schedule tasks that require a lot of thinking. Plan your day so that the types of tasks you need to complete are done when you are most likely to feel up to them. If you feel like you can't do something properly, you're far more likely to put it off.

Finally, make sure that your day includes scheduled breaks and that you take them. Taking time away from complicated tasks, studying or anything else actually makes you more focused when you get back to work.

Analyze the Problem

Part of my job, for a very long time, involved bidding on big government projects. Often, the project's bid documents would be bound in several inch-thick volumes, with drawings and addenda, all cross-referencing each other. To say it was daunting was an understatement. There were hundreds of pages of complicated jargon and technical terminology, sitting in a corner, ominously.

When you look at something like that, it's only natural to look for excuses not to jump in.

But there's no way to get the job done other than to get started.

Before I started doing anything else, my approach was always to take the time to summarize the information in the document.

I would list the work scope and specifications, make notes on questions that needed to be asked, and read the contract's general and specific conditions.

It may seem like a waste of time and counterproductive to take the time to do that before you actually start working on the bid. Still, those few hours actually made everything else a lot easier. Because I knew what I was getting into, it was all a little less scary, and I knew where to start. I could make my to-do lists and plans better and had a much better idea of how much time the whole project would take.

Abraham Lincoln was quoted as saying, "Give me six hours to chop down a tree, and I will spend the first four sharpening the ax." It may initially feel like a waste of time, but it always pays off to "sharpen your ax" first.

If you're procrastinating because you're facing a seemingly momentous task, take the time to do the same. A few hours upfront will save you a lot of time, effort, and frustration later on.

Fake It till You Make It

If you're putting something off because you're afraid of what might happen when you do it, you probably feel like the proverbial deer in the headlights. You can see the lights coming toward you, but you're too scared to move, so you can't even get out of the way.

The funny thing about fear is that usually, you can fake your way out of it. So many people who speak in public are terrified, but they simply pretend they're not, plaster a big fake smile on their faces, and do it anyway.

Remember being the new kid in school? You took a deep breath, walked into the class, and pretended that everything was fine. Soon enough, other kids were asking you about yourself, and you realized that it really wasn't as scary as you thought after all.

Many things in life are the same way. No matter how daunting the task is, if you just take a deep breath, take the plunge, and get started, you find that it's not quite as big a problem as you thought it was. In fact, you might even find that you start enjoying yourself.

And if you don't? Well, you've lost nothing, and you're no worse off than you were before you tried.

Trim the To-Do List

It's always a good idea to keep a master list of all your tasks and goals. If you tend to procrastinate, though, you might find that looking at hundreds of things you need to get done makes you feel defeated and like you might as well not try.

Instead of setting yourself up to fail, go through your tasks or goals at the end of every day, and write down a shorter, more realistic daily to-do list.

Include five of the most essential tasks that you really must get done and another five that would be nice but aren't critical. Get the five critical ones done first, and if you have time left, tackle any others you can. Whatever is left on the list at the end of the day can go onto the other list too.

Make the tasks on your list smaller and more manageable too. If marketing your business is a priority, for instance, focus on getting one social media post done every day. If you need to start exercising, schedule at least ten minutes of physical activity into your day. It's hard to find an hour, but everyone can manage ten minutes!

Your to-do list should allow you to get things done, but it should also set you up for success.

Do One Thing at a Time

Yes, we've all been told that multi-tasking is the way true rock stars get things done. But most of that is not true.

Studies have shown that when you try to concentrate on more than one thing at a time, nothing gets enough attention, and everything falls a little short.

Instead of trying to do ten different things simultaneously, spend your days in blocks where you focus on one thing at a time. Start by checking your email. Then update your to-do list accordingly, and then start tackling one task at a time off your list.

Even if you don't finish a project in the time allotted, you will get far more done, and the results will be higher quality if you just focus on that one thing for 45 minutes or an hour. Try it. Time yourself, concentrate single-mindedly on one thing, and see how much you can achieve in a very short time frame.

Create Accountability

We've already mentioned telling someone (or several people) that you trust about your goals and your plan to beat procrastination. Now take it a step further.

Create penalties for missing your goals and have your "accountability partners" hold you to them.

For instance, if you miss a critical task, goal, or deadline, you must pay money into a penalty fund. Make a deal with them that if you get to a certain amount, you'll take them out to dinner with the money. Not only does having someone else hold you accountable make it harder to break promises you make to yourself, when there's a penalty, there's also an added incentive.

Even giving yourself time limits to get a task done and then setting a timer with an alarm can help keep you on task and prevent your mind from wandering.

Consider Your Environment

Sometimes, it's not really procrastination that's holding us back. It's all the distractions going on around us. The key to getting more done and having fewer excuses not to, is to create environments designed for productivity.

If you find that you're easily distracted by noise, try to work in an area with a door you can close or get a white noise machine or noise-canceling headphones.

Turn your work area away from hallways or windows where you might be distracted by things going on outside. A blank wall is not stimulating or exciting, but it's great for keeping you focused on the task at hand!

If you work in an office environment, don't feel bad to hang a do not disturb sign on your door. If you need to get work done, there's no time for chit-chat. But make time to catch up with your colleagues too. Relationships do matter – as long as they're not an excuse to put off important projects!

Sometimes, it's not work or things at the office that we procrastinate about. You may have personal projects you are passionate about or dream of completing, like writing a book, building a blog, or something else. Our environments also play a huge role in these situations. You may find that your home is just too chaotic, and you can change your setting there as also. Take your laptop to a library or a coffee shop where life won't interrupt you every few minutes and put in an hour or two of uninterrupted work.

You would be surprised how much you can achieve when you take all the distractions out of the equation.

Ban Technology

Technology is not the enemy or the root cause of procrastination. In fact, as you will see later in this book, there are several technologies designed to help you get more done.

Still, it's strange, that even though we have so many tools and gadgets that are supposed to let us get more done, very often, they do the exact opposite. That's usually because we are already predisposed to procrastinate. These tools just give us another excuse to avoid the things we really don't want to do right now.

If you're always answering emails as the notifications pop up, turn off notifications and only allow yourself to check email three times a day. First thing in the morning, around lunch, and before you leave. Everything that can be sent by email can wait a few hours, and if not, the person who sent it will almost certainly call you.

Phones are hugely distracting, too though, especially smartphones. Make sure that everyone who might need to reach you in an emergency has your office or landline number, and then keep your phone in a drawer, your brief-case, or purse. You can check that three times a day as well, and the world will not end. Guaranteed!

Try to avoid social media and online news sites. These apps and sites are specifically engineered to keep us actively using them and have us subconsciously addicted. We've all started to watch a YouTube video or read a listicle and then looked up three hours later after seeing far too many pugs and cats and wondered where the time went! Social media, news, and online videos are a black hole, and if you fall into them, you might only emerge hours later. Just don't allow yourself to open those sites when you have things to do.

When you are prone to put things off and procrastinate, you're always going to tend to look for things that will give you something else to focus on. You know what they are, so be proactive and take them out of the equation.

Remove All the Excuses

You may not even know you're doing it, but when you put things off, what you are really doing is making an excuse to put something off. You're giving yourself permission not to do it.

"I'll do this tomorrow. I'm just too tired today."

"I can't do this yet, because I need Y to do Z first."

"I am upset, so I can't start my diet today."

There are endless possibilities when it comes to making excuses, and you've probably got pretty good at it over the years. You probably even have people in your life who allow you to make those excuses. We're very good at finding the people who enable us in so many different ways!

If you're going to succeed in becoming proactive rather than a procrastinator, you need to remove as many of the excuses as you can. It's time to really realize and accept that the only person you control is you and that the buck always stops with you.

If you need something from someone else to get things done, then it's up to you to get it from them or find a way to work around it. If you are always too tired or too busy to get things done, then you need to adjust your schedule.

Excuses work for a while, but eventually, even if you're still making them, people will stop believing them. So, look for the things you can change, rearrange or remove from your life, so you can get the things you commit to done.

Drop the Busy Work

If you have too much to do and not enough hours in the day, it's time to take a closer look at what those things are. If they're not worth your time, they may just be another way for you to avoid things you don't want to do without feeling guilty about it.

Consider how much you earn per hour in your job. Chances are, if you're a skilled person with a few years' experience behind you, you're not doing too badly. Now consider that if you're spending your time doing relatively simple tasks like filing, sending faxes, or following up payments, you're being paid considerably more than someone who could do that job as well, or better than you can.

This isn't only true about work. We do this in our personal lives too.

Instead of taking advantage of people and services designed to handle the tasks that take a lot of time but deliver very little value, we insist on doing them ourselves. Or maybe we insist on doing things the hard way. Whatever it is you're doing, if you're doing things that take longer and "cost more," you're guilty of busy work.

Look for more efficient ways to get things done, delegate tasks that are time-consuming and low value, and clear your schedule for things that really deserve your attention.

Help Yourself

As you will undoubtedly have noticed, this chapter is very much about getting out of your own way.

Everybody finds excuses not to do things from time to time, and that's okay. Still, if you're a natural procrastinator, you're a master of the art. If you're honest with yourself, you know what you do to give yourself an "out." Just stop doing them.

Don't schedule things for times that you know you won't want to do them. Don't invite distractions and small talk that you know will get you off task. Make sure you're comfortable, not hungry, and able to focus.

If your schedule is crazy all the time, and you don't have time to think or breathe, take a long hard look at the things on the list. Chances are at least some of them could be done as well or better by someone else, a paid service or some type of technology. Use those options, free up time, and get more done.

You're great at getting in your way. Now you need to become great at setting yourself up for success.

Self-Reflection

Are there some people in your life that you
trust to be great accountability partners?
Name up to 3 people who would be great at
holding you accountable.

In what environment are you most productive?
How could you best create or be in this space
more often?

TIME WASTED IS EXISTENCE; *USED* IS LIFE.

- *Edward Young*

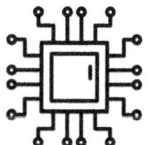

EIGHT

Tools & Technology

While technology is undoubtedly a big distraction these days, it can also be a big help. We've collected some of the best tools and technologies to help you plan your days, keep you focused and on track, banish distractions, and more.

Many of these are free to use or have a free version, but some on this list are commercial products. We've included them here so that you can make informed decisions, but we can't recommend one over the other. Take a look, see what works for you, and hopefully, they'll help you get more done.

Planning Tools

Having a plan for each day, week and month is a big part of getting more done and getting things done on time. These are some of the tools out there that can help you to do that.

. . .

Outlook Calendar or Google Calendar

Let's start with a simple one that you probably already have on your computer at home and in the office. Microsoft and Google's calendars are a great place to schedule your day. You can add meetings, invite other people to collaborate, and share your calendar. You can also have different calendars for different things, so you can have one for work, one for home life, one for fitness goals, one for studies, and so on.

Both of these options are also available online. So you can access them from anywhere via your Outlook or Google account, and you can set reminders, access it on your phone, and more.

Trello

Trello is a project management tool that doesn't look like a project management tool. In fact, it uses "cards" that are sort of like digital sticky notes that you can move around as needed.

You can create various "boards" for different things, so again, you can manage your work, studies, and personal life in the same place. This is great for simplicity, and you can add and edit cards easily. Trello lets you collaborate with other people too, and because you can drag and drop cards as needed, it's great for people who work best with visual tools.

Trello is a commercial software, but there is a basic free version, so you can get started and try it out without paying a cent.

Asana

Asana is another productivity/project management tool that lets you create various tasks and milestones, set deadlines and reminders, and change the status of items. You can also share projects, tasks, and milestones with members of your team and collaborators if you choose to.

Asana works a little more like a traditional project management tool (but without the complicated Gantt charts project managers use!) It's also a commercial software with a free version, so you can try it out and see if it works for you.

Web and Media Blockers

Social media, news sites, and videos are time thieves. But there are several ways you can block them so they can't interfere with your productivity. Many of these are available for desktops and phones, and there are options available for most browsers and operating systems.

Freedom

Freedom is one of the best-known web and media block-ers. It works on pretty much every operating system and on all kinds of devices. It's also very flexible.

This software lets you choose what you want to block and for how long. So, for instance, if you still need to access the web for work or a project, you can simply block social media and other sites that suck you in and steal your time. You can choose to block them for up to eight hours too, so for your whole workday if necessary.

You can also choose to sync your settings across devices, so you can't be tempted by your phone or tablet!

Freedom also has free and paid options, so you can try it out to see if it works for you.

Self-Control

If you're a Mac user, you can download a free application called Self Control that allows you to block specific websites for set periods of time. But beware – it's designed so that once it's installed, you can't disable it – even if you delete the application!

If you use Windows, you can try an open-source equivalent called Self Restraint, which does the same thing.

Cold Turkey

Cold Turkey is another web blocker, but instead of only allowing long chunks of web-less time, this application allows you to schedule in mini-breaks during the day when you're allowed to check-in and see what's happening.

That's particularly useful if you find that rewards work well for you. If you know you can check your social life support in an hour, you'll be far more inclined to buckle down and get the job done!

They also offer three different services: Blocker, which is just for blocking websites. Writer, which "turns your computer into a typewriter" so there are no distractions. Lastly, Micromanager which allows you to limit applications you can access – so no more sneaky games!

There's a free version of Cold Turkey and a pro version with a one-off payment.

Time Trackers

Sometimes, the problem isn't that you're losing time, it's that you have no idea where the time is going.

You sit down at your desk, ready to work, and hours later, you're still there, not much is done, and you don't know why!

Time trackers are a great way to figure out what's eating up your day, so you can work on strategies to limit those things. There are several on the market, and again, many have free versions. These include:

- Toggl: It is a cross-platform time tracker that lets you track how you use your time online and off.

- Clockify: This is another time tracking option that allows you to track and enter how much time you spend on each task.
- Timecamp: This is another free option that you can use to track time on work-related apps. If you know that you're wasting time elsewhere, you have a better idea of what you need to do to stay on track!

Time trackers might seem like an extra step in your already busy day, but just like keeping a food diary or a spending log can help you to identify problems, so can tools like this. Even running and using one for a few weeks can help you figure out what you need to do to stop distracting yourself, and that's a big step in the right direction.

Focus Booster

Focus Booster is a part-time tracker but also offers so much more. It automatically records what you're working on and does timesheets for you. It has a built-in timer so you can break your day into time chunks and get more done. It has a "mini timer" to count down to your next break (great if racing the clock motivates you!)

This application is also cross-platform compatible, so you can use it everywhere.

There is a free trial for this software. Still, even the paid versions are only a couple of dollars a month, so it's very affordable.

To-Do Lists

Writing things down, creating checklists, and then checking things off are hugely beneficial in keeping everyone on task – no matter who you are. Lucky for us, technology has taken us past Post It Notes on the computer monitor (although, if that works for you, stick on!)

If you are looking for something a little more high-tech, try these.

1-3-5 List

1-3-5 List is an app that makes it easy to pare down your daily to-do list so you can focus and get more done. This is how it works:

- Every day, you choose one big, three medium-sized, and five small tasks to accomplish.
- By forcing you to choose and categorize tasks, the app actually makes it easy to prioritize.
- As you complete tasks, you can digitally check them off the list.

The application is cross-device compatible, and there's a free Chrome add-on.

MOTIVATION IS
WHAT GETS YOU
STARTED. *HABIT*
IS WHAT KEEPS
YOU GOING.

- Jim Rohn

Afterword

Everyone procrastinates and puts things off sometimes. But if you're finding that it's a recurring theme in your life, you have a bad habit that you need to break. You will never reach your full potential until you admit that you're part of the problem and start taking steps to change the way you approach tasks.

People procrastinate for many various reasons, and it's rarely just because they're lazy or don't want to achieve. In fact, it's usually the exact opposite. Maybe you already have too much on your plate. Maybe you're terrified of success, failure, or change. Maybe you aren't even entirely sure that you want to do the things you're putting off.

Some people simply think that they're scatterbrained, forgetful, or easily distracted when really, they're doing all of those things to give themselves an excuse to avoid things they don't want to do.

But the reality is, once you've taken on a task or set a goal, you're committed to getting it done. If you often find that you have to do things you don't want to do, you might need to take a closer look at why you're agreeing to do them. You can always say no, but if you don't, you need to take steps to get it done.

Like everything in life, beating a procrastination habit starts with admitting that it exists. You have to acknowledge that you do this and what your triggers are. Without knowing those things, everything you try is likely to be less successful, and you might start thinking that you're stuck with this problem. You aren't.

Since so many people who procrastinate are high achievers and perfectionists, you might also need to change your idea of success. You might not succeed in your goals or get everything done on time every single time. But you don't have to. Even if you can manage 90% of the time, you're still going to knock it out of the park.

Procrastination might not be the worst of the bad habits, but if you don't get a handle on it, eventually, it will catch up to you.

The good news is that you don't have to hire a therapist or a life coach to make these changes. If you're honest with yourself, you know why you do this, and you know the types of things you are prone to do it with. You can make the changes needed to stop putting things off and get them done. You can set yourself up for success. Nothing is standing in your way but you.

You're never going to deliver the best quality results when you leave things to the last minute. You're never going to have the life you want, or lose those ten pounds, or make those changes to relationships that will make you happier.

You have limited time to get everything done. Stop putting things off, grab life by the horns, and find out what you can really do! There really is no time like the present!

IT IS EASIER TO
RESIST AT THE
BEGINNING THAN
AT THE END.

- Leonardo da Vinci

Thank You

Thank you for taking the time to read this book.

If you've enjoyed this book, please let me know by leaving an Amazon rating and a brief review! It only takes about 30 seconds, and it helps me stand a chance against big publishing houses. It also helps other readers find my work!

Thank you again for your time, and have an awesome day!

Resources and Links

There are countless other research papers, articles, and programs out there that are devoted to procrastination. That's not surprising because there are estimates that as many as 20% of all adults are chronic procrastinators. Many more admit to procrastinating from time to time. You are not alone, but that doesn't mean you can't use some more information!

If you need to read a little more about why you procrastinate and how you can work to keep yourself focused, these are some great resources.

Psychology Today

A good resource on procrastination, what causes it, and what you can do to stop letting it affect your life.

https://www.psychologytoday.com/ca/basics/procrastination

Why Wait? The Science Behind Procrastination

An in-depth look at the causes and effects of procrastination by The Association for Psychological Science.

https://www.psychologicalscience.org/observer/why-wait-the-science-behind-procrastination

Procrastination or 'intentional delay'?

How to tell if you're procrastinating in a way that will have a negative impact or if you are delaying something in a potentially positive way.

https://www.apa.org/gradpsych/2010/01/procrastination

Procrastination: An emotional struggle

A closer look at the hidden causes and triggers of procrastination.

https://ct.counseling.org/2019/10/procrastination-an-emotional-struggle/

Procrastination Resources from The Center for Clinical Interventions

A page operated by the Australian government, offering a variety of information and resource to manage procrastination.

https://cci.health.wa.gov.au/Resources/Looking-After-Yourself/Procrastination

The Procrastination Research Group

A 20-year research project by Carleton University in Canada. Read various research papers and media stories related to the science of procrastination.

https://www.procrastination.ca/

On the Behavioral Side of Procrastination: Exploring Behavioral Delay in Real-Life Settings

A research paper/report on the behavioral patterns of procrastinators by a Norwegian research group.

https://www.frontiersin.org/articles/10.3389/fpsyg.2018.00746/full

Technology makes procrastination easier but it's not the cause

A report on the relationship between technology and procrastination by Maclean's magazine.

https://www.macleans.ca/education/university/technology-makes-procrastination-easier-but-its-not-the-cause/

Psychology of Procrastination: Why People Put Off Important Tasks Until the Last Minute

A report published on the American Psychological Association website looking at the root cause of procrastination.

https://www.apa.org/news/press/releases/
2010/04/procrastination

The Paradox of Procrastination

A look at some of the false beliefs that drive or allow us to procrastinate and how we can avoid them.

https://www.psychologytoday.com/ca/blog/fulfillment-any-age/201204/the-paradox-procrastination

New Data Shows That Most People Are Too Lackadaisical About Their Goals

A Forbes report on the true prevalence of procrastination, which may be much higher than reported.

https://www.forbes.com/sites/markmurphy/2018/12/27/new-data-shows-that-most-people-are-too-lackadaisical-about-their-goals/

Made in the USA
Las Vegas, NV
11 April 2021